Bangalore

Dear Bill,

Thank you so much for your kindness, your enthusiasm, and your grace. Much love to you and Dolores.

11/11/16

KERRY JAMES EVANS

Bangalore

COPPER CANYON PRESS

PORT TOWNSEND, WASHINGTON

Copper Canyon Press is in residence at Fort Worden State Park in Port Townsend,
Washington, under the auspices of Centrum. Centrum is a gathering place for artists
and creative thinkers from around the world, students of all ages and backgrounds, and
audiences seeking extraordinary cultural enrichment.

LIBRARY OF CONGRESS CATALOGING-IN-PUBLICATION DATA

Evans, Kerry James.
  [Poems. Selections]
  Bangalore / Kerry James Evans.
      pages cm
  Poems.
  ISBN 978-1-55659-405-2 (PAPERBACK : ALK. PAPER)
  I. Title.

  PS3605.V36824B36 2013
  811'.6—DC23

                              2013010571

COPPER CANYON PRESS
Post Office Box 271
Port Townsend, Washington 98368
www.coppercanyonpress.org

Acknowledgments

I would like to thank the editors of the following publications, in which these poems first appeared, some in slightly different versions:

AGNI: "Seven Chants, A War Cry"

AGNI Online: "A Year or More"

Beloit Poetry Journal: "An Empty House," "Leaning in from the Sea," and "Packed in Ice"

Briar Cliff Review: "Canaan"

Copper Nickel: "The Deployment"

Court Green: "Blue Ribbon Tomato Soup"

The Dos Passos Review: "Siphoning Gas"

Eclipse, A Literary Journal: "Monopoly"

Florida Review: "Lilacs and Razor Wire"

Fugue: "Colloquium"

Harpur Palate: "Soldier's Apology" and "A Treatise on Violence"

Iron Horse Literary Review: "Design" and "Sisyphus"

Narrative: "Cold Porridge," "Elegy for the Kudzu Vine," "Embers," "Hanging Threads," and "An Instance of Love"

New England Review: "A Good Hunt"

New Letters: "Blanket Party" and "Volcano"

The Pinch: "Waiting for Fire"

Poet Lore: "Grown Men" and "What Makes the Green Grass Grow"

Spoon River Poetry Review: "Operation Noble Eagle"

The bangalore torpedo clears a path 10 to 15 feet wide through barbed wire entanglements. In minefield breaching, it will explode all antipersonnel mines and most of the antitank mines in a narrow foot path. Many of the mines at the sides however may be shocked into a sensitive state, which makes extreme care necessary in any further mine clearing.

—*United States Army Field Manual, 5-25: Explosives and Demolitions*

Contents

Bangalore

Lilacs and Razor Wire

Bent over in a folding chair, my arm a rag of oil,
I scrape the carbon from my M16
with a pipe cleaner here in the armory
named after a young colonel
                                    who hanged himself.

No one sitting here really knows
whether or not the colonel
was a homosexual.
I bring up my mother-in-law,
                                    who is.

Outside the window the local convicts
have decided to mow down the lilacs
blossoming along the roadside.

We go back to talking about homosexuals
and homosexuality, and I say:
We are all a little gay, which lands me
on the floor in a wrestling position.

                    *

Seventeen, April: the month
of five flats, skittering
down freshly graded
limestone gravel roads
in my '92 Buick LeSabre,
picking up a nail, stopping,
pulling out a four-pronged tire iron
and hydraulic jack
(having learned
from the first four flats),
and changing the driver's side
front tire amid a downpour.

*

I was learning a common necessity:
how to change a tire *and* be on time
to roll dough at Little Caesar's.

*

Trigger on the stock, chamber
and barrel, those convicts
mowing lilacs, my own hands
greased on the weapon.

I think of my mother-in-law,
who called New Year's
with a message for my wife:
I will always love you, hon.

Cape Cod. Winter. People
leave the Cape this time
of year. I don't know
if it was loneliness, but

my wife's mother turned up
a bottle of pills and swallowed.
I would say more, but I wasn't there.
I can't give the image.

*

But perhaps those pills began in the pistils of flowers,
and perhaps those flowers are these lilacs.

*

There was nothing we could do, but we drove
the fifteen hundred miles to Cape Cod anyway.

We took the old US highways, a full moon
blueing the mountains around us.

We slept in the hospital until she recovered,
until she divorced her wife

and said that if she could do it all over again,
she would have stayed married to my wife's father.

                            *

But on the trip out there,
my wife called the mountains gods.

                            *

I let her and I drove,
the lilacs dead,
having yet to blossom,
this M16
in my hands
buried beneath the moonlight,
stashed in the freezer
with my youth,
and when we
popped a tire
and my wife asked
about the dark,
the North Carolina
State Penitentiary
tucked behind razor wire,
Do we have a flashlight in the trunk?
I told her no,
but I have done this before.

                            *

I pulled out a jack and tire iron, and I lifted our car from the road,
the words I offered of no use, so I asked her: *Kneel with me,*
our hands numbing on the lug nuts, the two of us, changing a tire.

I

Aegisthus: Exiles feed on empty dreams of hope.
I know it. I was one.

—Aeschylus, *Agamemnon*

An Instance of Love

        Reader, it doesn't matter what you think happened to those wheat fields
reaped by the slow
           threshing of steel.

I wouldn't consider the possibility of mice.

        Nor would I remember a childhood disease,
    a drop-off point,
             or even the multicolored
                ball pit
                    of ketchup and syringes.

Children are a grandparent's dream.
We were never so young.

        You and I have harvested nothing more than the stench
           of middle age,
dropped here by a stopwatch
           and a bottle of Gatorade.

                        Refuel.

Electrolytes are popular in psyche wards.

Our lives are no more our own than a philosophy
is to a room crowded with ego.

Be still.

Imagine a silent waltz begging you to me. Our shared anger

                              falls free from skyscrapers,
             cracks the glass walls
                  we create sipping wine
                          on the river Thames.

                  I've seen ghosts bear crosses that ribbon from blood,
          then stiffen,
                      like a sword pulled from sand.

Think peach wood burning in a burlap sack.

             Think oil. My hair.
             Your well-painted nails.

             My cell phone.
             Your ear.

             Our conversation one-sided
             as always, the

chickens swallowing
their chicks' bones
in an aluminum shed.

You are as lonely as I am.

I have seen you crawl between your sofa cushions
and read the lines
given to your hands.

Even I have been known to pray.

Even I have run my palms
across the carpeted walls
of the local bowling alley,
and I admit
I have looked
at the woman
behind the counter
renting shoes—

this, while keeping a picture
of my wife folded in my wallet,

not that I
would forget
my vows,
                            but that I might.

Reader, how I would love to request
your presence at my home for a game of darts.

                                    I am not your child.

                        Nor am I the smoked ribs
                    cooling under
                        a poplar or a
        Gatorade bottle crumpled
                    on the side of your driveway.

                        I mostly think of our conversations.

        I imagine the space between a wrecking ball
and a brick facade
                    millimeters before impact.

                        We'd do well enough
                                    to occupy that space.

Operation Noble Eagle

I failed at being my grandfather, the man relieved
from service by flat feet—what carried him
to the county dump to sift through junk

for profit at the Saturday night auction
in Jasper, the town where I was born.
And somehow I remember leaving

the hospital in my parents' married arms
while two squirrels chased one another
outside a window. But that was long ago,

not the summer I handcuffed two soldiers
my age who, driving drunk, attempted to barrel
the gate in a Dodge Ram—all pipes and smoke.

It was July. I had guarded the north gate
at Fort Leonard Wood for eight months:
can of mace, nine millimeter dangling

from a holster at my hip. I recited Yeats,
climbing that gyre out of six years'
service in the Army National Guard.

Guarding what? I searched Peterbilts
with a Mag-Lite—what the army
called *Operation Noble Eagle,* ribbon

pinned to the breast pocket of my dress greens.
Like any soldier, I spit-shined boots,
pressed collars with steam and starch,

while my fellow Democrat and bunkmate,
Lieutenant Bradley, slipped paychecks
into sequined thongs at Big Louie's.

I drank coffee at the Waffle House.
On occasion, I flirted (like my grandfather)
with waitresses. Each worth the two-dollar tip.

Do not think I have not buried my fair share
of Hummers up to the doors in mud.
I bulldozed mountains to mounds,

stuffed C-4 in a picket, secured
makeshift bangalore with duct tape;
do not think that in training I did not blow

a Missouri forest to an Afghanistan cave.
More than not, I miss basic training,
the private with Tourette's blaspheming

drill sergeants. A line all to himself,
Daniels marched where he wished,
so long as he shot expert and passed

grenade training. He lost his leg to an IED.
Civilian translation: Improvised Explosive
Device: cell phone trigger, and without

armor-plated vehicles, Daniels noticed
his boot torched in a ditch, a boot
similar to what my brother and I burned

in the projects as boys. We'd set fire to it
with matches I picked up at Jitney Jungle
after crossing an electric fence—after buying

groceries with my mother's food stamps.
But I am wrong to claim this story.
This story might belong to any soldier

left behind. Lieutenant Bradley
asks an Iraqi schoolgirl for a bathroom.
Soldier with a weak bladder, he pisses

every fifteen minutes, can work a room
in five languages; I taught him one,
and he might understand the art

of being poor, having to send Daniels
home, and for a month, a hero
among friends and community locals,

but Bradley e-mailed yesterday to say
Daniels shot himself after the parade
rolled away. Bradley wants to attend

culinary school now, his master's
in political science of no use to him.
He asked me to help develop a menu.

I told him I am married but will try,
and to send my condolences
to the family. But he knows that I

am married—that the word *condolences*
explains more than the difference
between our uniforms, the years

he's put in and the years I've been out,
my uniform hung in the closet with my boots,
a card standing on the fireplace mantel

at Christmas from a family I never met,
and this poem is for every dead American.
This poem is not for anyone who reads poems.

Waiting for Fire

1

I stepped barefoot down cement, blood-bugged porch steps,
bloodsucking—
                I stepped off home into cow pond muck.

Tadpoles lurched between my toes,
a catfish sliced my heel, a swallowtail
tore through a willow.
                And while the dogs marched down the drive,

a Confederate flag whipped its pole,
an old wind
           working its will on this land.

2

I root a fence as if I might understand the rot,
a junkyard drowned in a rebel yell—
fifty acres left to cousins and distant relatives.
They stand in a pine thicket, shaking their rifles.

3

Sunday dinners after brimstone—
blasphemy in the bones
—a backwoods dialect

beats a horse with the stock
of a Civil War musket.
Look at these tongues beaten to sand.

4

Sling-bladed gravel roads,
shotgunned signs,
praised His holy name

at a cemetery,
an unknown
soldier, a mass grave.

5

I hurl cow patties from pasture to pasture,
spade a grave for Jack, my hunting dog.

Watch me lay a blanket over his eyes,
watch him wither beneath red clay.

6

I walked Highway 129 from Yampertown
to Brilliant, stuffing
Walmart bags with aluminum cans.

I climbed the red banks
of my childhood and once,
without thinking of leprosy,

grabbed an armadillo by its tail,
the hayfields dried and waiting.
I looked at the foothills of Appalachia.

7

                    I waited for fire.

8

My grandfather would pour gasoline
onto the leaves and light a match
beneath his oaks—this before he greased
bacon and fried the house to the ground.

Two heart attacks, three strokes,
halo screwed into his head,

and the intensive care unit,
one-hour visits a day. Our conversations

lost to cancer. And what do I remember?
This man sipping orange juice
from a plastic cup. I remember
peeling back the lid and holding the straw.

9

Antebellum double-wide barreled down the drive
in halves, the insides wrapped plastic—

stapled shut. Our home jacked up on cinder blocks,
I dug a three-inch trench

for the underpinning. I nailed blue rock to press board.
We moved the piano in first. Half-pressed

keys and lazy strings. The oak encasement
my brother and I held, strays pacing the tree line,

barking at the bulldozer, leviathan of earth,
fumes breaking from a steel pipe and tin can lid.

10

Gray sky, antler rattle, salt block and deer lick.
Behind the blind.
Kickback.
Buck knife across the throat. Drag. Hang.

11

Water to my knees, deep enough to tube
two miles through mountain passes,
Appalachian rock crashing beneath me,

vacation, a short drive to Tennessee,
through Georgia sometimes, foothills
resting their moon-cast blue backs,

vertebrae stretching like knotted rope
—my mother's favorite braid,
and her childhood caught up in a mountain

cabin, while her father bought roasted peanuts
from a roadside vendor selling produce.
She remembers him peeling a peach

with his bone-handle pocketknife—what I
lost last year curling apple skins from their core.
Strange seeds clipped ground.

A garden moved quickly downstream,
slipping into grooves of deer piss,
undertow—

and the minnows followed the current
back to where we settled. I follow
the seeds as far as I can, but I lose them.

I throw the knife into the river
where it sinks into the gravel bed,
and I can't get it back—it's buried

in the river and the seeds have emptied
into the ocean or planted
themselves somewhere along the bank.

12

Where am I in all of this nostalgia?
The river is a liar. It will give you nothing.

Sisyphus

The winter I abandoned Guin, Alabama,
I left its projects—a conglomeration
of 1960s governmental housing
passed by Congress to maintain
the needy and ignorant. Barbed wire
ended a potholed asphalt road,
and on the left: our apartment, mud
running up the side, staining the brick,
and in the yard, the rusted springs
of trampolines stretched limp
between the few needless patches
of switchgrass, where my brother
and sister piled into a red wagon.
I'd pull them up the hill. No sooner
than we'd reach the top, I'd hop in
and steer the three of us down the road.
One day our hollering interested
an old couple sharing a cup of coffee
on their porch. *Baby oil. You need*
baby oil on them wheels. You'll see.
Of course we needed baby oil.
We greased the wheels on that wagon
and flew like hell, until we had mangled
ourselves in that barbed wire,
throwing a wheel into a snake bed.
Walking here, now, fifteen years
later, I think of Sisyphus
and what he might have said:
Get up and climb that hill,
before you lose track of your lives.
And he would have been a wise man
to say such a thing. That night,
my father drove down from Hamilton
to ask about our collision.
My soon-to-be stepfather spat tobacco
into a Mountain Dew bottle,
my mother standing in the doorway.

Halfway through the interrogation,
my father buckled. My father
spat in my mother's eye.
I'd like to say the two men
courting my mother in their own ways
fought in the living room,
but these were southern men:
egalitarian—men of the backhoe
and the tiller, gardeners of a common
Alabama childhood. From the couch,
Glenn told my father: *That is enough*—
what I hear echoing off the asphalt.
My mother moves into the kitchen,
wiping spit from her eye. *This is a family*,
I tell the wagon rolling down the hill,
my brother and sister filtering
into their rooms, my stepfather
shutting the front door. I ask for violence.
Instead, these men cry, my arm
broken—the right arm of my father,
stitches in every room of the house,
and in the yard, the wagon's shattered
wheel, my knowing that I have nothing
but this cast holding it together.
My father: nothing but his spit to offer
my mother. And today, I leave a house
crying at the bottom of Alabama,
and in the yard where I left my brother
and sister, the whites still hang
from the clothesline, and beneath the wire
from where we'd swing, a child
digs at a root with a spade. He stabs
the ground, then waves, pointing me
away from that home, and there I am,
drifting up the hill with my father.
I am pulling an empty red wagon.

Packed in Ice

My wife   pulls a peach   from   the freezer,
then   stares   at the knives   stuck

in their wooden   block.   I want   the right   line
for our   marriage,   but the exact   emotion

is a peach   packed in ice.   I cannot accept   this,
though   clearly,   here   it is,   cold

and ripe,   and now,   in hand,   passed
between us   like a desperate   artifact.

Elegy for the Kudzu Vine

It's time somebody did it right, unwound you from your immortal trees,
from crucifix-style power lines
and pulled you from the roots, doused you
in diesel fuel and burned you in the ditch where you rest.

Effigy of myself. Effigy of anything but Alabama
and Alabama all the same, boiled peanuts
rotting green on a gas station counter
outside Montgomery, reminding me of you, and how you cling

to life: one tendril coiling a pair of posthole diggers.
Maybe I should take the vine
that you are and wrap you around my hand.
Call it bareback brass knuckles on a Saturday night,

talking to a man who goes by King Snake, another Catfish,
in a bar where they name me Cotton,
my skin shining through a pitcher of Miller Lite.
We talk pussy. We talk railroading.

We talk about a giant chicken formed by the welding of mufflers.
We talk about how a milk pail from 1942
rusts behind the smoker.
Hog jaw. Rib cage. Pork butt pulled slowly with a fork.

But never do we talk about the vine that grew between our toes
in the churches where we were baptized,
those county roads the graveyards of our childhoods.
We throw darts. We drink cheap beer from small glasses,

stumbling over the line. We hold God in one hand and swear with the other.
We'd give anything to forget
about the one-stoplight towns, Piggly Wigglys, the BP station
where we bought Mountain Dews after football practice

and a Snickers for the road. We'd give anything to understand
what you have done for our lives, how you hold dead trees
from falling after an ice storm,
how you keep red clay from washing into our veins—

all that iron and blood. There is no forgetting when raised the grandchild
of the Ku Klux Klan. And you, old vine,
tied like a noose as a reminder, blooming your purple flower
so that every hanged soul might find a voice.

But even we know the power of tithes, King Snake
pulling a five-dollar bill from his bifold wallet
and making change, lining stacked quarters
on the pool table like deacons ready to receive an offering.

With a bent cue, he shoots, recalling, with each ball he sinks,
a dead man's grin, each ball the color of a sin.
I ask Catfish to take over. It is here,
I learn the speech of men. The speechless guilt of every swig.

I've never shot pool worth a shit, but I know the crack
of a pool stick when snapped.
I know a splinter in the throat. I know blood
tastes better when it's dried to a busted lip and why Moses

parted the Red Sea, that the Old Testament is better than the New,
because it is filled with the blood of men
and the wrath of God, that a vine is not the truth,
but a placeholder for a history not worthy of remembrance.

An Empty House

1

Oak limbs sprawl into the   windowpanes,
and the unpainted   picket fence—

fallen over.

Soldiers washed under   the sand.

No, there are rats crawling about   —chasing squirrels,
wallpaper sagging

across the floor
like the necks   of men in old age.

I own nothing but my   teeth.

I will never learn   it all.
I am   better for it.

2

No children running about this house.
No ghosts.   But the ghosts

     of soldiers.

What of the air-conditioning units   stalled
for who knows   how many years?

They rust like   rabbit cages
holding shredded   newspapers and hay.

The brick and mortar   foundation gives way.

Outside the screened-in porch, across   the yard,
this oak's roots sprawl   —like

that wallpaper, like those   necks
I have seen drooping   from my jaw—

there,

a white dog   with a brown spot for an eye
barks at the tails   of the rats

     —at me.

I trace the lines of his barking.

     A soldier.

3

My neighbor told me   of a poker bet.
He told me of how   this home—

he told me how this house   was bought.
No, he told   me how it was won.

When I walk through this house, there   is
no family   sitting at the table.

There is no   table.

Only the rats   circling the unpainted
picket fence,

my eyes   bloodied like maples turning—

and who lived   here?

Who lived   in this empty house?

I must   live here, though I

have never owned a thing, but   my teeth,
this winter with no snow—

locked out,   this family.

Are they walking down the sidewalk?

When I am   hanged.

A soldier is   buried beneath this   house.
The floorboards creak his name.   Mine.

Siphoning Gas

Once, I got the Ford to run—'66 Falcon.

Siphoned enough gas from the mower
to get me to town. Stopped at the college
campus—watched girls walk to class,
home, wherever, while an eight track
blared Led Zeppelin.
                              I was a bad
motherfucker, toilet paper splotching
my razor-nicked chin.
                              But I kept my chin
to my chest. The girls didn't care.

They wore pigtails and short skirts—
all of them could have passed for sixteen,
but they didn't.
                              They didn't notice
the music, the leaking carburetor,
or the ticket slapped on my windshield
for parking without a permit.
                              And that was okay
—I got what I went for: a moment
away from that yard and summer
of black snakes and rabbits chasing
one another in that thicket grown
high in the middle of our two acres
of Missouri—carved hillside,
forty-five-degree angle, I swear
to God,
              though I did have to repeat geometry,

and I pushed a self-propelled mower
that didn't self-propel—twice as heavy
as a twenty-inch-blade Murray—
but I built my arms, my abs stone.

In such good shape, sometimes

I would run down the five-mile stretch
of gravel to the river and watch floods
come and go—'93 the worst, but I saw
nothing of it.
                    I still lived with my brother
and sister and mother in the swamps
of Mississippi and a prayer that whatever
happened in that blue-striped Falcon,
magic, hormones, a night of steamed
windows—whatever it was, love, maybe
that brought me into this world, I don't know.
I just wanted pistons to fire in that four-barrel engine.

Leaning in from the Sea

—a line from "Oysters," by Seamus Heaney

Too much black in that boy, she tells his father, shears in hand.
Too much ears. Too much nose.
Not black: Pussy.

But the bitch is too white.
She's a one-room trailer
at the bottom of a gravel pit.

She was hot shit, high school cheerleader—
she was prom queen material.
Too white. Too trash.

Too slow to keep up with them boys.

*

We ran the ball up the gut.
We only won when it rained.
Senior year, we went 3–8.
I fucked a girl.

*

Fucked the green out of her eyes
and now she walks around brown and blue.

The boys at the trailer plant in Brilliant call her Texas.
I don't know why. She never married?

She plays tambourine
in a country band Brandon Franks formed.

*

They tied me up for a traditional buzz cut
fit for a football player. Fit for a soldier.

We'll make that cowlick go away, boy.
We'll train your hair to lie right.

*

Last time in the city, a pigeon
splattered its innards right next to me.

Who'd do that? Who'd clip
a pigeon's wings

and throw it at a person?
All that blood. All those feathers.

*

Sounds Roman. Sounds like soldiers again. Sounds like trumpets.

*

Religion has always been a coin in the mouth.

*

In D.C., Mother said, *Don't you stand up for yourself.*
Don't you go getting in trouble. I don't care what for.
You'll be dead, boy. You'll be dead before I'm thirty.

*

When I lived in the city, which I did, I learned phrases
mean less when you're holding a gun.

*

Which I am.

*

When I lived in Mississippi, where there are no cities,
only snake pits and psychics,
I learned young mothers bear children
out of necessity. Out of loneliness.
That cotton always needs more hands.

*

No need for the combine, boy. No need for the gin.

*

You won't make it around here.
You got wide between your eyes.
You got something wrong with your gait.

*

Always leaning in from the sea.

*

When I'm called back to the front.
When the living forget their families.
When bone dust and blood inherit the land.

*

Who will open his own stomach like a Roman?

*

I am holding a gun.

A Good Hunt

Blackberries rot in a cornfield across the road,
and where blackberries rot, so do men:

orange-vested and gun-toting, retrievers
their only hope for a good hunt.

Their salvation: the scattering of birdshot
—the blood on the ground.

*

I do not believe in hope or salvation or men.
I am not a hunter, but have hunted,

dressed myself to my environment,
drifted landscapes

between cypress and saw grass.
I have tailored swamps to fit my needs.

*

From behind a blind,
I pumped a mallard with a twelve-gauge.

*

The quail drop from the dogs' mouths
and the hunters' hands,

and these men bind the quail
with nylon rope, leave my porch view

swearing, my own camouflage
pulled tight against my arms.

*

I, too, am prone to kill, set cratering charge
to hillside, let clods of dirt

lift like geese and plunge—
steel pellet strike feather and heart

—collapsed lung, outstretched wing,
neck limp in the cloudless dawn sky.

*

The skinning of any bird,
the hanging and the blood-drip.

Blanket Party

Because Private *Shit-bird* Jenkins
wore underwear in the shower,
we camouflaged soap in pillowcases
and marched single-file
to the first platoon barracks.

The fireguard slept. We were all of eighteen.
We strapped Jenkins to his bed
by the four corners of his blanket
and we beat his body.
I rammed a sock in his mouth.

It was a quiet beating without
cadence. The next morning,
Jenkins showed our work
to the drill sergeants. They
smoked us. We stood, hands

out to our sides, for one hour.
There was no mail call.
When asked to address the company,
Jenkins declined, kept
his bruises beneath his boots

and BDUs—looked at us, Third Platoon
—our motto: *Third herd—last in line,*
first to die. The drill sergeants
gave Jenkins the go-ahead.
Fired up, he marched us to the pit.

We learned hand-to-hand combat,
throwing our merciless bodies
against recycled tires and sawdust,
each of us taking a shot in the gut
from Jenkins. I spat blood,

asked for more. I called him a faggot
who couldn't fight, and since
our heads were shaved to fend

off ticks and lice, I didn't pull
his hair, only planted my elbow

into his temple. He passed out.
One month later, he was discharged.
The barracks blackened with sleep,
and that darkness was broken
by a bugle. We'd killed our own.

Soldier's Apology

1

What apology would my mother give—my father,
a room of doubt, where excuse evolves to reason?

*

My mother turned forty this year. My father
forty-two. I am currently eight years older
than my mother when she had me.

When my father was the age I am now,
I was six—old enough to fire a gun.

*

When I was born, my father joined the air force,
then the army, moved his family from the South
across the world. He swore I would never see
Jasper, Alabama, again.

*

You cannot escape your family. You cannot escape
the South, Alabama, Golden Eagle Syrup,
the quarter horses in your uncle's barn,
or that goddamn clay red as your wife's hair.

This is what I tell myself, living in Illinois.

2

Why don't we take it outside, walk it to the lake
—drown it?
        Tie a cinder block to its ankles—
                no, that hardly makes sense.

Planning never has been my strength.
I get it from my father, the colonel marching
troops into Baghdad.
            I am one of them.
You are one of them.
      We are all marching into Baghdad.

      Jody is fucking your wife.

Your sixteen-year-old wife, my sister, pregnant,
                belly out to here.

She is carrying a baby boy
        who is also marching

into Baghdad, *Persia, the last beast to fall,*
the pastor yells from the pulpit.

             *

I would rather kill you than apologize to you.

When I say kill, I mean wrap det-cord around your face,
stuff your ass with a bangalore torpedo, stab a crown
of barbed wire into your head—make you wish
              you could be reborn.

3

We are the dying multitude.

*

If you see my mother, my father—tell them
I followed my orders.

                    I carried the guidon.

Engineers lead the way!

*

But you will not see my parents, and you will not know
them. I will not know them. We will not see one another
beneath the flares, rockets, tracers, mortars, grenades
tossed in our foxholes—we will not stop killing to say

I love you.

*

To our wives—to our mothers, our brothers, our sisters,
our fathers:

                    We are not sorry for killing you.

Volcano

I've seen the Mojave, but I've never seen the desert.
In training, I swept for mines, but I've never seen

my brother's leg destroyed after detonation;
I've seen the legless soldier walking with a prosthetic

across town, through the grocery store, at drill,
trying to hold on for one more year, for pension.

I've seen the different phases of training—crawl,
walk, run—and I've seen the failure of battalions

at each phase. I've cleared a path, myself,
and marked, with flags, the safe zone;

and I've walked through such a minefield.
I've witnessed the Volcano, a machine, scatter

960 antitank mines
over one kilometer of sand, but never have I

seen the battle, or the desert, or those mines, or TOC
calling a precision-bombing air strike across the line.

I've dismantled many mines, winnowed Russian mines
from French mines, but I've never seen the mines

on television; I've known soldiers who have seen
those mines; soldiers caught under fire, blasting cap

clenched in the mouth, jaw gone missing;
and that must be what it means to see the desert:

a face charred, blood dried and stuck to bone,
the land laid out before you erupting.

What Makes the Green Grass Grow

A military man wraps his fury
in camouflage. Concealed,
the man must feel at home:
ordered, pressed, complete.

That is the point of a uniform—
to look sharp in garrison,
to salute the brass properly
without a wrinkle showing.

And what of the sewer grate
that catches in a soldier's mind—
bolt and chamber—spark
pouring from a fresh M16

in fresh hands with fresh ideals,
firing bullets down a range
of plastic pop-up targets
that fall facedown in dirt

with each hit, only to spring
back to the way they were?
After a day of shooting,
the maggots chant: *Blood*

makes the green grass grow,
affirming the natural order,
as if smoke and lead are tools
for planting in the afterlife.

II

And he went forth unto the spring of the waters,
and cast the salt in there, and said, Thus saith the Lord,
I have healed these waters; there shall not be
from thence any more death or barren land.

—II Kings 2:21

Monopoly

She is always the wheelbarrow—a piece
he can't grasp. He is the cannon.

They never deal out property; the Deluxe
Edition, they'd rather fight with each roll

over New York and Boardwalk, Railroads
and Utilities. He's yet to own Boardwalk,

but he manages to swindle the Railroads.
Occasionally, he is lucky to land in jail,

where he doesn't have to mortgage property
to pay rent. She buys hotels early, casts

him to the ghetto of Baltic. Once, he boasted
three monopolies and won Free Parking.

They place $500 in Free Parking. He bagged
his earnings from the middle, revealing

the mustached man with his shoulders
shrugged, hat tipped. The man winked at a stack

of pastels tucked under her edge of town.
The game was fixed. She kept drawing

the good cards from Community Chest
and Chance. Her husband lived in the suburbs

and she was his landlord. Like his father,
he slipped off and got drunk on Boardwalk,

gallivanted for a while. It cost him everything—
she owned that, too. Fed up, he took out a loan

at 10 percent interest, paid her and passed Go,
collected two hundred dollars and made a run for it.

He got as far as Pennsylvania before she caught
him stealing her hotel shampoo. Clogged

barrel, she broke him. She gave the worst smile:
Cook me supper and I'll let you stay.

Colloquium

Here is the lamp of my marriage: slender and green,
a fluorescent bulb to save energy, and the base:
dust collecting into a gray mass that is my hair,
my new Chrysler—American-made, and to prove it,

a sticker on the driver's side rear window: *Built
with quality and pride by UAW members at the Sterling
Heights Assembly Plant*, which is enough for me,
though Sterling Heights sounds as generic

as the store where I bought this lamp, the blue-vested
man explaining energy efficiency. And I can't figure
out which I hate more, the person, or the phrase
energy efficiency: nasal in sound and paradoxical

in nature. No, listen. Energy means life, spirit,
emphasis. Efficiency: the ability to produce
the desired effect with a minimum of effort,
expense, or waste. What is sterling about a city

supported by a car plant? My car is an abomination,
and the fluorescent bulb lighting my room
is an elephant on Silk Road; efficient at what?
Gas prices are down. A recession has taken hold.

I've made some plans, and they start with this lamp,
a box of hair dye, and my car. These three things
are all I need to get laid, and I'm not talking
about my wife—I'm talking about Sterling Heights.

A woman working the line, tired after work,
drinking a beer with the guys at the bar, and yes,
I'm hitting on her at that bar, and the guys
give me a look. I've got it all planned out.

I ask her what she thinks about these new hybrids.
She says, *They're not bad.* I agree. We walk out
of the bar, leaving the guys, leaving the beers
on the table, and I ask her to quit her job

and move in with me; I'm kicking my wife
out of the house. I hate our lamp. And the lady
says, stepping into my car, *These Sebrings*
are pieces of shit. Come to find out, she drives

a Toyota. And that's fine. In Blue Springs, Toyota
just opened a plant. There must be a formula
for car plants and communities: lame adjective
plus general noun—the particular language

left for the owner's manual, which is where we
are, flipping from one page to another, looking
for directions on how to operate the jack,
how fast to go on a donut, and she says to me,

You're leaving your wife? And of course I reply
that I'm not. There's nothing in the Declaration
of Independence that leans toward compromise,
only the absolution of what makes us plain,

and I want her right now, in this new car
on this new and glorious day. I want my wife
to watch, because she and I both know we're living
together under the pretense of lower car insurance

and half rent. This is the first marriage, ruined
based on the same principles that give young people
in college the courage to believe they can major
in anything, when their parents know well enough.

They raised these children, heard them developing colloquial
speech patterns. *And you want to study microbiology?*
Very well. I have no plans to visit Sterling Heights,
and I'll never squeeze a bottle of dye on my hair.

Neglected Questions

I. Lead

Foreshadowing the apocalypse, I leap from one stage
to another—raindrops on a white canvas, cat

                              under the car,

moonlight and a walk three hours away.

                    Earlier:

changed the burnt spark plug, jumped my wife's car,
and spoke with a homeless man about the war.

                              On his right hand,

a bullet.

                    *

After he pokes lead, he takes my arm,

                    Get out.

I nod and fold my beret into my cargo pocket.

II. Jar

Lying there with no shirt, his spit-shined boots
collapsed over the end of an air mattress,

                              my father dreams;

about me,
              I do not know—

probably his current wife and kids, who live
farther down the road

                    than he likes to admit,
or his parents:

              Tater Knob, Alabama,

football growing up, where he was all-conference his senior year,
but too small to play for the University of North Alabama.

His mistakes roll with his eyes;

                          they are peas locked in a mason jar.

III. Salute

My wedding ring is bent
from when I threw it.

                The stones did not fall out.

I forgot to separate the laundry.
The teacups are dusty.

           Leave it alone.

Let us sample wine on a Missouri hillside, grapes and a sunset,
let us raise our glasses, salute the snow geese and that forever V.

I am a good shot.

           Next week, I will kill the leader.

IV. Neck

Our wedding took place in a Greek amphitheater; we rented columns,
and you gave me a marriage,

                    yet this morning I wake
with my hands—copper tubing

                    coiled around your neck—
a boy slammed into the wall,

                    piss streaming down my legs
and off the ends of my toes—

                    the warm drip staining our Persian rug.

V. Foil

What about a picnic on wheat, turkey, cheddar,
no news,
            a clear sky, shade?

Who cares about the temperature or pollen count?

I want kites and Frisbees, a dog
chasing his leash through the park,
not grease on pavement, a kiss
and the office.
            She crumbles foil: *Will you remarry, if I die?*

VI. Circling

My brother breaks a crappie's jaw, the years
                              a lure weaving among cattails and muck,
where memory follows a white line to truth:
                              taut stringer, seven fish the size of my hand
hanging beneath a canopy of circling dragonflies,
                              limbo hooked to a drowning, felled willow.

VII. Classicism

An afternoon nap then coffee.

                Clorox and small circles

in the tub at midnight.

          Was lonely.

Sweat and Vivaldi.

        If it were Country,

                I would be my mother.

*

This morning, in the same room: Renoir, Monet, Van Gogh, Cézanne.

Maybe that is why I took a nap, where shipwrecked,
I learned meter from Homer, love from Sappho.

Over my shoulder, *Scrub harder.*

        My mother has never seen
        a masterful brushstroke—
        tasted an orchid's scent.

Steel wool scratches porcelain:

        Clean has nothing to do with dirt.

Blue Ribbon Tomato Soup

This is dinner: tomato soup
with black pepper and garlic salt,
a grilled cheese buttered
                         on both sides,

charred in the skillet on the stove.

He serves his brother and sister this meal
with napkins and plasticware.
                              They say grace.

Their parents are working.
Parents work.
                The meal is superb.

He gets a wink and a high-five, turns off
the stove eye—
                    sometimes he forgets.

He is a chef at any restaurant imaginable:
Cracker Barrel, Country Kitchen,
the coffee shop on US 78,
just before the peanut shack
in Carbon Hill.
                   His brother and sister agree.

They say he ought to enter the county fair.
Drape a cloth over his arm
                      when he serves.

They remind him not to speak about how
food stamps paid for this meal.

They talk about the neighbors up the hill,
the expiration date on the milk jug.

Design

And this, canvas of paintless
numbers, this square, it
is the square
of my imagination, four
corners and seam
running from this
middle, my mother's awful
trailer, the children
she keeps in a day care—
a square day care, where I look
back into memory and recall
the driest of squares,
an empty pan
of meatloaf, ketchup
crusting in our stomachs
—my brothers and sisters
and all the children mothers keep.
And I think of the square world
and how it stumbles
down the stairs of space,
while we square off the yard
to plant seed, to remind
our children of what they
cannot have, while we
sample wine from a boxed
bowl, its drip
dripping on the tile floor
of this, our grouted design.

For the Popped Collar

Some asshole wearing cowboy boots
and a T-shirt tells me my popped collar
reminds him of country club pukes
from his hometown: St. Louis, MO,

a greasy stain on the back of an oil man
sipping The Glenlivet in some clubhouse,
the left-breast embroidered logo an eye
for the upper class, and this popped collar:

it must signify a whiff of toilet rot trailing
cedar baseboards from the bathroom door
at the VFW hall, where the commentary
began. And this is not the first time

I've encountered a drunken local
at a VFW hall. In Charlotte, I learned
what a double-tchotchke meant: two polos
standing at attention for Nixon—

stacked one on top of the other, like the logo
itself—a rider striking a white ball
from a pony—one of four players.
We'll say he's playing Three,

the most difficult position on the field,
and he's just passed the ball to Two,
who scores a goal, and that all of the players
in this scene are wearing the same polo

I'm wearing at this VFW hall on a Friday
night, a polo with a popped collar, stiff
with starch, a tuxedo-folded tip, with me
failing to mention the use of popping a collar.

It keeps the sun off my neck, I tell my beer.
But now I'm explaining fashion/style?
to the bartender, who is the son of a veteran.
We explore the structures of class.

When does one decide to wear the collar
popped? Is this a question of philosophy?
We agree to go no further when he
kindly asks me to leave, until he discovers

that I served six years. He offers to buy
me a beer. I think of history, the origins
of polo traceable to Iran as cavalry training
for the Persian army: up to one hundred riders

per team. I invoke the bartering system
of my European ancestors. I offer him
a lecture on the necessity of language
and he asks: *Language? I just don't like your collar.*

Why do you wear it like that? I don't answer him.
Rather, I listen to nineteenth-century British
imperial officers practicing military
maneuvers, riding those ponies, shod hooves

galloping down the night street. Then I see
my father, camouflaged collar weighed down
by a maple leaf. He's trying to call from Kosovo.
He's found the highest mountain. He's looking

down at the village. He sounds out the words
for village—*Ovo sehlo*—but this is a language
he keeps failing to pronounce. My cell phone
is ringing in his ear, and he's standing

in the Balkans, waiting for me to pick up.
He's leaving my name to the wind.

A Treatise on Violence

Mad cow, the nurse said, *ravaged Europe from 1980 to 1992.*
For ten months of 1988, I lived in England with my family.

I cannot give plasma.
At five years old, I ate cannibalized beef.
My brain might be eating itself.

I cannot give plasma at the plasma center
where, in a raffle drawing of people
who have donated twice this month,
one person will win a plasma television
worth four-hundred-fifty dollars.

I asked the nurse how the British
owning the plasma center
had anything to do with my brain eating itself.

You can never give plasma or blood.
And when will my body become meat for my mind?

*

Tangoed in the living room beneath the ceiling fan
with my wife and six beers and polka music
and two helpings of dinner—walked outside,
looked off the deck at the sun casting shadows

of a tree on a garage door, pack of children
howling at a playground—Saturday
a football day, helmet to helmet, an upset;
Colorado beat Oklahoma, Auburn beat Florida.

This, the day men watch bodies that were their own.
But I have this dance waiting after this cigarette;
I have a shadow and voicemail from my father:
he counts gravestones at Gettysburg.

*

We were stationed in England—my family.
The playground was installed
at the end of the cul-de-sac
of our neighborhood three weeks
before we moved to the Azores,
the next stop on my father's route
to satellite command headquarters—
Pentagon, Washington, D.C.,
contractors, revolving door.

But I am talking about a playground
and skinned knees, riding my BMX
into a European-looking van—
I was flat-nosed and weak,
like my younger brother,
the high school football-stud-graduate
working part-time toward an electrician's degree.

There are wires in the machine
—*Neutral is white, but white,*
he says, *is not always neutral.*

*

I'd like to give a retirement plan
to each member of my family,
tell them to live their lives, invest
in nothing—the poor do not belong.

I am poor. I play golf on Mondays
with used clubs, drive a used car
to a public course and hit a used ball
to a hole after striking the ground

with the club head more times
than my father choke-slammed
me to the wall, more times
than my father choke-slammed

my brother to the wall. No promotion
and I strike at an already scarred
and filthy ball. My father is honest.
What apology does a father owe his son?

*

I hate golf, but the walk is nice—bullshitting with the guys
about nothing, football glory extended play-by-play—
we drop out of the pond without counting the stroke.

I am not angry at my father;
                    I am not angry at my brother.

The crazies in the plasma center are not angry
at their condition, their fucked eyes
swirling in a room
                    of free coffee, peanut butter crackers,

a movie about football—volume turned low enough to sack
the waiting room, the nurse calling loudly the names
of high school dropouts,
                    marriages that began at eighteen

at a courthouse with two witnesses—

*

                    I do not belong here.

*

Tube-drawn from a long needle, my wife's blood
drains, her plasma the muddy yellow of urine.

                    She collects her twenty dollars.

*

If I am mad, where, but in the shadow of a tree
that has lost the leaves of its crown
                        and buried roots in winter,

a tree crossing a power line
and shucking its bark,
this sycamore standing in my yard?

And now, I will dance the mad dance with my wife,

bow before her curtsy, archaic
and chauvinistic
                —what she appreciates when she takes my hand,
                                        asks me to lead.

I cannot be angry, so I swing my wife
across the room.
                Her red hair unfurls like a scroll.

Canaan

> The river turns on itself,
> The tree retreats into its own shadow.
> —Theodore Roethke, "The Far Field"

Walloped between railroad ties and gravel,
my brother and I shouldered burlapped rocks
from a pit we thought the underworld,

and we dumped those rocks in an onslaught
of forgetting on the train tracks, while light
caromed through a colonnade of idealized trees,

what we claimed Canaan, borrowing from the gods
our philosophies, the existential as reasonable
as the grave. We were tracking adolescence

across wilderness, seeking the impractical
—the shepherd snug at harbor,
eclipsed by the broadcast of a ham radio

operation snaking through our walkie-talkies.
To shortwave ourselves across space,
we might have sustained transmission

to other planets without risking a whipping
at home via iron skillet or hickory switch.
As sure as we walked, the interference

channeling our bodies, the train shook loose
the tracks, and our feet picked up quick,
the belly of the beast breaking on the shore

we called the living—those tracks where we
walked with fossilized rocks, wandering
nothing more than Alabama, with its thorny bushes

and quicksand, its acres of red clay farmland
lost to industry, carried on a train we could not derail.
Radio waves pulsed through us like our blood,

like the plows pulled by mules we knew so well
from the stories of our parents—as oblivious
to the coal cars as we were to the invisible world

we knew as the radio, what we might tune
our ears to for a bit of goodwill preaching,
a brazen loss of self, backsliding wolf-of-a-man

worshipping a whimsical cloud. It made sense
then—as much as anything does to a couple of kids—
looking out at Canaan, proclaiming the promised land.

Plundering

You start up Ole Maude and we take gravel to all your hangouts: the coffee shop,
        the iron bridge,
and your favorite, the county dump, where you found the stove Grandmother
        cooks supper on today.
Except for that back left eye, the thing works fine. I helped you clean it.
        We meet Cecil

at the coffee shop, where he pulls mints from his pocket—he thinks
        they go
with everything, and you let me know quick that coffee is good with nothing else
        but coffee,
yet behind your back, I've been stirring in cream and sugar for years.
        I don't drive a pickup

like you did, but I'll take the gravel roads to the bridge where you
        jumped
from the top as a boy, and when I'd ask if I could jump, you'd say no.
        I understand now,
but since you died, I've leapt several times into that snake-infested water.
        The current

took hold of me one time and sent me nearly a mile from the bridge.
        But I'm dry now,
and Ole Maude's waiting. Nothing beats a couple of Swisher Sweets
        to give you cancer
and a Chevy Luv to send you to the dump. Plundering's harder than it looks.
        Just because I've grown

two feet since the last time we've come out here doesn't mean I can see it any better.
        The smell is worse
and the caffeine doesn't hold as long. So I pop a mint in my mouth and breathe
        in the stench anyway,
but I don't find a stove or anything like it, just junk, piled up and buried,
        from someone else's memory.

A Year or More

I was never taught how to blow my nose.
Your nose, my father tells me, *is not your own.*

I ask him what this means.
He replies, *America.*

*

I watch my wife pluck her eyebrows,
shave her legs.

A woman loving herself
—what I never saw my mother do—

what my father would not allow,
young in his marriage.

*

America: first-class stripper with a space program,
bladed lawns trimmed to the sidewalk.

*

My wife knows nothing of stumps
—drilling the hole, pouring the gas.

Waiting, a year or more,
for the corrosion, the eating of the roots.

She knows nothing of hooking that stump
with a hoe and pulling it from dead clay.

The Deployment

Not in this lifetime, she said, so he walked her downstairs
and through the front door; he told her he understood.

He watched her leave. *Good-bye* stuck under his tongue,
the taillights, the warm air pushing from the gulf—

there, on his front porch he connected two constellations
he had forgotten the names for, and with that same finger,

he flipped them off, as if he were from New York or L.A.,
and he felt satisfied with his direction of the night sky.

He walked inside, opened a bottle of Scottish ale, *Belhaven.*
The beer was smooth. The beer was creamy. The country

he had always known as his own became an island.
He walked from one end to another, claiming a lamp,

the down comforter. He embraced the simplicity of this.
In the crook between the refrigerator and the cabinet,

the universe began to show itself: a mouse had fallen
for the peanut butter, the metal latch

and spring snapping, collapsing around the neck.
Though he did not see this happen, he imagined death.

He thought of his own death; he thought of the sea,
and then he stopped thinking altogether; *A mouse,*

he said to himself, *a woman.* He threw the beer bottle
into the trash along with the mouse, and he took the trash

to the curb. *She will be back,* he thought, but he wasn't certain.
He closed the door behind him and walked to bed. He wept.

Grown Men

I-90, my cousin carrying a load into Montana
on a pot of coffee, his rig broken down
with two flat tires, jack busted and the tool truck
buried in a snowstorm outside of Billings,

and this is obesity: stuffing doughnuts
with energy pills, pissing in a gallon milk jug,
while a CB strangles his cab; he thinks
he'll pull one off, thumbing *Tits Paradise.*

And this is no cliché from a horror flick.
This is a man who once was a boy,
every bit of five-feet-seven blocking
on the offensive line; he takes the poor girl

with a crush four years his junior to the prom,
a girl still sitting on the bus, still circling town.
He's not thinking of her. He's dialing me
from the bottom of his call list—a number

almost forgotten, save our conversation
at the last Christmas dinner, when he said,
We ought to catch up more often. A year later,
with winter set in, his name blinks on my phone.

We're grown men; there is no requirement
for our speaking to one another, but I answer.
I remember us throwing a football: '92 blizzard,
my grandmother's backyard of sod and clover

covered in snow. He describes the cold,
and what can I do? I imagine my tires chained,
clomping beneath me, Missouri icing its banks,
my cousin holding a candle to keep warm.

Cold Porridge

Sebastian: He receives comfort like cold porridge.
—Shakespeare, *The Tempest*, Act II, Scene I

For our time machine, we've gathered four helicopter blades
bent to ovals and painted pearl,
a widow standing center of the contraption.
She asks, *Why should I see my husband?*

*

Which is charming.
But she's never eaten cold porridge.

She calls it oatmeal like most Americans.
She calls a microwave *microwave*

and uses her microwave
to warm water for her oatmeal.

*

I have only the assumption our galaxy
resolves its alpha and omega in our time machine.
If not, I'm wasting my time.

*

Since women live longer than men, they must be smarter.
Carthage defeated, Roman aqueducts
were built on the principle
that water sustains the health of a population.

*

A lie, but true.

*

I've been called a misogynist.
Nothing comforts me.

*

Junkyards are time machines.
Widows are time machines.
Therefore, junkyards are widows.

But let's say I found the widow
in a junkyard. What of our
syllogism? Our middle term?

*

When I die, I hope my wife will not wall
herself up like all the women in my family,

recalling familiar stories over the holidays.
She won't. God knows, she won't.

*

I like the cold answer, the flat, cold truth of it.
I like a woman daring death.

A woman—who does not bury a husband
in vain—mourns awhile and moves on.

*

Last night, the widow called me on my cell phone.
Apparently, I am abusive.

*

She told me, *Your wife's pregnant belly will be popped with a fork.*
My wife likes that image: *Popped with a fork.*

*

But a crashed helicopter doesn't remind us of anything.

*

We can't know love without our forgetting:
the lore of a bone broken in three places—
a widow listening to another widow.

Myself.
The hospital room of beeps and buttons.
Widows will ignore you. Quiet forgetting.

Hanging Threads

Don't look at me like a boy.

                         Don't look at the overalls buckled

over my nipples,
or me hanging threads by clothespins
in a backyard lost to dog shit
                      and armadillo holes.

Look at my hands.

Look at the dangerous fold over the line,
the briefs of my family
an offering to gods
who would never set foot in this yard,
                          the chain-link fence

rusting under pine,

my mother salting pork chops in the house,
where a grease fire and an overdose
                       will knead her brain

then roll it like corrugated tin.

Here, the trenches I dug for a sewage line
run down a kudzu-covered hillside,
where we dumped two Fords and a washing machine.

A football I couldn't catch.

Look at my hands unpin board-stiff threads
from the line,
                    my long glance at my brother and sister

growing young,

climbing the half-filled propane tank.
                              Look at my hands.

Look at the fork that fed my mother,
                              the laundry basket,

stiff, folded clothes
stacked and spilling over the sides.

Grass clippings collect under my heels
and the pine needles have fallen—every one.
Look how cold I have become.
                              I was a boy.

Seven Chants, A War Cry

I

You nothing of a reader, this is the savage age of battleships and bombs,
candlesticks and underground shelters—

                    the radio address:

flare, satellite plowing a cornfield, caught mouse
and the dead ramparts we sing,
the movement from doubt to inquisition.

These are mornings roosters eat eggs, ant colonies gasolined—
tortured, the queen dead, her neck noosed and hanged.

                I am not your Savior. I am not your King.

II

Three men and a dissolved government
walk into a bar, order three drinks
and a shot apiece, ask the bartender—

prophet on a cliff seeks water, tree, wind—
and yet the notes keep that light, keep
that supermarket rolling to the abyss,

this trapped tile of bathroom soot,
this Rocky Top cracked down its spine,
this savage age, this day keeps moving.

III

Hear that headboard slap this wall, drop its studs
—hear these studs slap that woman, slap
that woman—

            let that woman's cry be the Iraqi cry,

the tribal cry, the ancient cry.

                              Break your shovel on your mother.

Pick up the ax and tear down the barn.
Burn it.
            Leave the field of Mars for the poor fucks to bloody up.

Drop the bomb. *Pick it up.*

                    Apologize.

        IV

Bow before yourself after dinner.
Bow before that chained dog.
The dog that runs as far as the link allows.

                    Chaining—   Chaining—

the dog chants.
                    The dog cries.

        V

Poured whiskey like nails.
Love was a red, red brothel
smelling of perfume, musk.

Men broke the bones
of their children—
thrust and sweat, thrust

and cry. The brothel was German
—the Nuremberg Wall.
On crutches, I paid

fifty dollars for a blow job.
Call my wife.
Tell her our marriage is lyrical.

Order the buffalo wings
and a Miller Lite,
tell me about the sacrifice fly

in left field, the botched
throw at home,
where you put to bed

your children—
who you give a teddy bear
to die in their arms.

     VI

Not when you know the end.
                        The children and fire hydrant

popped open with a wrench—
                        Look at all those hands and feet!

Who will be the first to go?
Let the mother speak first, holding a spatula.
What's that?
              Let him play?

                        Rusted water breaks the skin.
                        They are lockjaw. They are innocence.

VII

If there is a heaven, I'd rather not see it.
I'll burn with my brothers. This age

has fallen—cell phone call from 747—
shock and awe—commercial

for a razor and its four, five blades
—counting down before the rocket

zips into space. Cape Canaveral,
Cape Carnival, Cape Cod

and my mother-in-law swallows
every pill she can find, like my mother,

and I suppose I blast it into space—
these half-truth lives, these lives

dangling on the edge of Earth.
We will all be driven back to the sea.

Embers

—St. Joseph's Island, Florida

Crab claws and salt spray, crooked tent posts and this gut-churning gulf.
Coals glow in the fire.
                    Islands, you call them,

each eye a blanket Rorschach pulsing against empty smoke,
the bats unloading their wings
beneath the palms while the sand fleas
bite our legs.
                    Waves distill the moon.

                    *

Monarchs migrate through the gulf's hand and their wing-beat dance
strips Orion's belt from his hips,
your legs cold against the sand, the flea bite
and the flesh wound,
                    your bite's red eye a coin on your ankle.

                    *

You ask if I married out of love.

                    *

Further inland, seagulls stretch their necks and cry.

                    *

Fire poke, ash cloud, the wisping sparks—
a shrimp hooked on my line.
I cast into blood-dark water
                    —this island caught in the jaw.

*

Swept into the dustpan, these ashes—this woman,
my wife's college friend—

                thrown from her car and drowned.

Her body destroyed.

The metal air, the Stop sign plugged
into the passenger's window,
the broken legs
         of a deer carcass crossed on the ground,

its tongue licking a double yellow line.

                *

If she could speak, she would give her body to the gulf.
She crawls back to us.

I pull a grouper in and she approves,
this woman—
          this poor, destroyed woman.

                *

                          Stilted homes.
These stagnant and swaying homes
stilted from Pensacola to Miami,
this damned gulf breeze, this damned marriage.

This night is colder
than I remember.
You watch the dead woman in the water.

I lift my reel to a black heaven
with a black mouth and think of my white,
conquerable sunburned skin rubbed raw on the white sand.

You move without me listening.
I think of the island shifting—a cat's tail lifting the sun.
The logs in the fire

have long since yielded to the sand,
and you have forgotten
to filet and fry the fish.

I leave you to your water.
                    I leave you to your dead friend.

                    *

Hoot owls beyond the shore, beyond the cracked back
of dawn, the hustling redbirds
and the silent road,
the fish-rot singing and the bones
—the ivory bones charred in the fire.

                    What have I forgotten in this cobalt tide?

                    *

These stories beneath this sand.
These Spanish forts bombarded.
This island as barren as its stilted homes.

                    *

Everyone has left me and it is cold and the tide creeps.
I have left the fire to burn out
and there is no wood, no fire, no matches
to make a fire, no flint, no home
to break into and you—
                    you have left me for your friend,

wading out knee-deep, the moon as faithful
as your freezing breasts,
your makeshift raft, the silent water
thrusting you back to me.

How can I take you back?

*

Carry yourself to me as you would carry a dying child,
swaddled and heavy.
Let your head drop onto my shoulder.

Forgive me for not saving your friend.

It was my fault.
It was also yours.

But where will the palms
dance with the pines if not in death?

Drink the saltwater from this insipid gulf
and look out over the water.

Cup the moon in your hands and be healed.

About the Author

Kerry James Evans served six years in the Army National Guard as a combat engineer, including one year of active duty at Fort Leonard Wood, Missouri, during Operation Noble Eagle. He holds an MFA in creative writing from Southern Illinois University–Carbondale and a PhD in English from Florida State University. His poems have been published in *Agni, Beloit Poetry Journal, Narrative, New England Review, North American Review, Ploughshares, Prairie Schooner*, and others.

Lannan Literary Selections

For two decades Lannan Foundation has supported the publication and distribution of exceptional literary works. Copper Canyon Press gratefully acknowledges their support.

LANNAN LITERARY SELECTIONS 2013

Kerry James Evans, *Bangalore*

Sarah Lindsay, *Debt to the Bone-Eating Snotflower*

Lisa Olstein, *Little Stranger*

Roger Reeves, *King Me*

Ed Skoog, *Rough Day*

RECENT LANNAN LITERARY SELECTIONS FROM COPPER CANYON PRESS

James Arthur, *Charms Against Lightning*

Natalie Diaz, *When My Brother Was an Aztec*

Matthew Dickman and Michael Dickman, *50 American Plays*

Michael Dickman, *Flies*

Laura Kasischke, *Space, in Chains*

Deborah Landau, *The Last Usable Hour*

Michael McGriff, *Home Burial*

Heather McHugh, *Upgraded to Serious*

Valzhyna Mort, *Collected Body*

Lucia Perillo, *Inseminating the Elephant*

John Taggart, *Is Music: Selected Poems*

Tung-Hui Hu, *Greenhouses, Lighthouses*

Jean Valentine, *Break the Glass*

C.D. Wright, *One Big Self: An Investigation*

Dean Young, *Fall Higher*

For a complete list of Lannan Literary Selections from Copper Canyon Press, please search "Lannan" on our website: www.coppercanyonpress.org

Poetry is vital to language and living. Since 1972, Copper Canyon Press has published extraordinary poetry from around the world to engage the imaginations and intellects of readers, writers, booksellers, librarians, teachers, students, and donors.

WE ARE GRATEFUL FOR THE MAJOR SUPPORT PROVIDED BY:

THE PAUL G. ALLEN
FAMILY FOUNDATION

THE MAURER FAMILY
FOUNDATION

NATIONAL
ENDOWMENT
FOR THE ARTS

Anonymous
Arcadia Fund
John Branch
Diana and Jay Broze
Beroz Ferrell & The Point, LLC
Mimi Gardner Gates
Gull Industries, Inc.
on behalf of William and Ruth True
Mark Hamilton and Suzie Rapp
Carolyn and Robert Hedin
Steven Myron Holl
Lakeside Industries, Inc.
on behalf of Jeanne Marie Lee
Maureen Lee and Mark Busto
Brice Marden
New Mexico Community Foundation
H. Stewart Parker
Penny and Jerry Peabody
Joseph C. Roberts
Cynthia Lovelace Sears and Frank Buxton
The Seattle Foundation
Dan Waggoner
Charles and Barbara Wright
The dedicated interns and faithful
volunteers of Copper Canyon Press

To learn more about underwriting Copper Canyon Press titles,
please call 360-385-4925 ext. 103

The Chinese character for poetry is made up of two parts:
"word" and "temple." It also serves as pressmark for
Copper Canyon Press.

The poems are set in Adobe Caslon Pro, with titles set in
Rockwell Extra Bold.
Book design and composition by Phil Kovacevich.

CPSIA information can be obtained at www.ICGtesting.com
Printed in the USA
LVOW03s0329010514

383963LV00004B/18/P

9 781556 594052